DATE DUE

DIOGENES

The Story of the Greek Philosopher

Told and Illustrated by

ALIKI

Prentice-Hall, Inc., Englewood Cliffs, N.J.

DIOGENES: The Story of the Greek Philosopher
Told and illustrated by Aliki
All rights reserved
Copyright under International Copyright Convention
Library of Congress Catalog Card Number: 68-28512
Printed in Japan

For Franz

Long ago,

in distant, ancient Greece, there was a man named Diogenes who dressed like a beggar and lived in the streets. Yet he became known as one of the greatest philosophers of his time.

This is how it happened.

When he was a boy, Diogenes lived in a town called Sinope. His father was a banker and the family lived well.

But one day, when Diogenes was grown, his father was accused of coining false money. He was put in prison and Diogenes was banished from Sinope forever.

Alone, Diogenes went to Athens.

For the first time he had no money and nowhere to live. He begged for food and slept by the roadside.

One evening as he sat thinking about his life, Diogenes saw a mouse scurrying about. He watched it and thought: "This little mouse is not afraid that night is coming or that it has no home. If it is hungry it goes and finds what little it needs to eat."

Then and there, Diogenes decided he would live as that mouse did, without the comforts of warm clothes or a place in which to live.

Meanwhile, he heard of a teacher named Antisthenes who said many of the things Diogenes already believed. Antisthenes said that in order to be good, one must live simply and accept hardships. Only then can one value the important things in life.

Diogenes wanted nothing more than to be Antisthenes' pupil. He went and told him so.

But Antisthenes would not teach just anyone at all. He expected his pupils to be poor and to deprive themselves of comforts. He wanted them to live according to their beliefs.

Although Diogenes was poor, Antisthenes refused to take him as a pupil.

Again and again Diogenes went to the master and pleaded.

Again and again Antisthenes refused. Once he even lost his temper and beat Diogenes to be rid of him.

But Diogenes only said, "Hit me. Never will you find a stick hard enough to drive me from your lessons."

At last Antisthenes realized that Diogenes
meant what he said, and accepted him as a pupil.

Diogenes not only learned from his teacher,
but lived the lessons he was taught. He dressed in rags.
He carried only a sack on his back and a stick in his hand.

In winter and summer, he walked the streets of Athens barefoot. He slept on the ground until one day he found a tub in the Temple of Cybele. He made the tub his home. It did not shelter him completely from rain or freezing cold or from the scorching sun. Yet Diogenes suffered these hardships willingly.

He ate what little he needed and often chose
to be hungry. Even when he was invited to a banquet
he was not tempted by the huge amounts of food.
Those around him marveled at his self-control.

Diogenes owned one bowl from which he ate. But one day he saw a boy drink from his cupped hands, and threw the bowl away. Even that he did not need, after all.

Sometimes Diogenes begged for food if he could not find any. He even begged from statues. "Why do you do that?" he was asked.

"So I will get used to being refused," he replied.

For there were many people who had more than they needed, but would not share it with those who had less.

Diogenes was an honest man and expected
everyone else to be honest too. He criticized those
who did not say and do the things they believed.

One morning he walked through the
marketplace carrying a lantern.

"Why do you need a lantern when the sun is shining?" someone asked him curiously.

"I am looking for an honest man," Diogenes answered.

He spent a good deal of time traveling around in Greece.

It was on one such journey that something happened to Diogenes that changed his life. He was captured by a band of pirates and taken to be sold as a slave.

This, too, Diogenes accepted.

"What can you do?" the slave merchant asked him.

"I can govern people," he replied. "Sell me to someone who needs a master."

A wealthy man from Corinth named Xeniades bought Diogenes, and before long he realized this was no ordinary man. Instead of remaining a slave, Diogenes became teacher to Xeniades' sons.

He taught them their lessons and many sports besides, for Diogenes believed that exercise was good for the body. And of course the children walked barefoot, like their master.

For the rest of his life
Diogenes spent his summers in Corinth
and traveled to Athens in winter.

He spoke to crowds who
came from far and near to listen to
him, and many of Antisthenes' pupils
became his own.

He was known and respected
throughout Greece.

One day as Diogenes was sitting by the roadside, the mighty king of Greece approached him. He had heard of Diogenes and had wanted to meet him for a long time.

"I am Alexander the Great", he said.

"I am Diogenes," answered the old man.

Though Alexander was a proud man, he was not offended. Instead, he wanted to prove his respect.

"You may ask of me anything you wish," he said. And Diogenes answered, "I ask only that you stand out of my sunlight."

Alexander was surprised to hear such an honest and fearless request. He knew of no one else who would speak so to his king.

"If I were not Alexander," he replied, "I would be Diogenes."

Diogenes lived to be an old, old man. It is said that he died on the very same day as the famous king whose respect he had won—Alexander the Great.

Now more than two thousand years have passed, but Diogenes is not forgotten. Indeed he is remembered as one of the wisest men who ever lived.